THE MAGIC COW

Retold by Claire Llewellyn

Series Advisor Professor Kimberley Reynolds

Illustrated by Anaïs Goldemberg

Letter from the Author

When I left university, I started work as a book editor. After a while I began to wonder if I could write books of my own. I could, and that's what I've been doing ever since. I mainly write about real things like dinosaurs and the Moon, but I've always loved fairy tales, too. Years ago I saw a toad trying to cross a busy road. I picked it up and carried it over. For the next week, I was half-expecting a handsome prince or a pot of gold. Sadly, nothing ever appeared!

The Magic Cow is a fairy tale set in Iceland. Frida, a young girl, has to face mountains, winds and wicked trolls. Three cheers for Frida, who is brave and clever. And three cheers for Bukolla the cow, who gives her a helping hand.

Claire Llewellyn

Once upon a time in Iceland, there lived a poor husband and wife. They had a small farm in the mountains, where they lived with their daughter, Frida.

3

The couple kept a beautiful brown cow called Bukolla. Twice a day, the wife milked Bukolla. Twice a day, the rich, creamy milk filled the bucket to the brim. How the couple loved that cow! To tell the truth, they loved her more than their own child.

One morning, the woman went to milk Bukolla. To her horror, the barn was empty. The cow had gone! 'Husband, husband, Bukolla's gone!' she cried. The two of them searched all day for the cow, but they could not find her anywhere.

That night, the couple were in an awful temper.

'Frida,' snapped her mother, 'tomorrow you must go into the mountains and look for Bukolla.'

'And don't come back until you find her!' growled her father.

Early next morning, Frida set off along the path that went into the hills. She was wearing a new pair of red leather shoes. On her back, she carried a bag of bread and cheese.

The path led Frida through a grassy meadow. Then it began to go uphill.

It twisted and turned around large rocks. It crossed a fast-flowing stream.

After an hour, Frida grew tired. She sat on a rock and ate some bread and cheese.

She decided to call to the missing cow.

Bukolla! Can you hear me, my dear?
Moo to me if you're somewhere near.

Far, far away, Frida heard a faint 'Moo'.
She jumped up and started walking towards it.

As Frida climbed higher and higher, the hills grew wilder and wilder. A waterfall poured over dark, gloomy rocks. Ice lay here and there on the path. After an hour, the girl began to tire. She sat down on a patch of grass and ate more bread and cheese.

For a second time, she called out to the cow.

Bukolla! Can you hear me, my dear?
Moo to me if you're somewhere near.

Once again she heard a 'Moo'. This time, it sounded louder. She jumped up and headed towards it.

Higher and higher Frida climbed. The sky grew dark with clouds and a cold wind began to blow. The girl shivered and hugged herself to keep out the chill. After an hour, she was tired again, so she sat down on a rock to rest.

For a third time, Frida called out.

Bukolla! Can you hear me, my dear? Moo to me if you're somewhere near.

This time, she heard a very loud 'Moo' which seemed to come from under her feet! Was Bukolla stuck in a cave somewhere? Frida jumped up and looked around.

13

Frida saw a wide opening in a rock nearby. She went through and followed a track that led down into a large cave. Her brave heart gave a leap. Bukolla, the beautiful brown cow, was tied to a ring in the wall!

Now, Frida was a smart girl. She knew all about the wicked trolls that live in mountain caves. So she quickly untied Bukolla. Then she led the cow back through the opening and the two of them turned for home.

The cloudy sky was darker still as Frida and Bukolla hurried back along the path. They had not gone far when they heard angry voices. Frida turned and saw two women behind her.

They were the strangest women she had ever seen. One was huge and the other was tiny. Both were ugly, fierce and strong. Frida knew at once that they were trolls. And they were coming after her and Bukolla!

Frida was shaking from head to toe. She cried, 'Oh, Bukolla, what can we do?'

Then, wonder of wonders, the cow spoke.

Pluck a hair from my tail, dear girl, and lay it on the ground.

Frida plucked one of Bukolla's brown hairs and laid it on the path.

The magic cow looked at the hair. She said,

> Hair, turn into a river so wide
> That only birds can cross to the other side.

Instantly, a huge river blocked the path between Frida and the trolls.

When the tiny troll saw the river, she stamped her foot in anger.

But the big troll said, 'I have an idea. Go back and fetch our best bull, and be quick about it.'

20

In a moment, the tiny troll was back with a magnificent black bull.

Her big sister led the bull to the river and the beast began to drink. It drank and drank until the river was dry.

Frida and Bukolla were halfway home when they heard voices again. Frida turned and saw the two angry trolls. They were getting nearer and nearer. The girl's teeth were chattering with fear. She cried, 'Oh, Bukolla, what can we do?'

Bukolla said,

Pluck a hair from my tail, dear girl, and lay it on the ground.

Frida plucked another hair from the long brown tail.

The magic cow said to the hair,

> Hair, turn into a fire so vast
> That only a bird could ever get past.

Instantly, a great fire blocked the path between Frida and the trolls.

The tiny troll was very angry and shook her fist at the blazing fire.

But her big sister said, 'I have an idea. Hurry back along the path and bring back the black bull. Sister, be quick!'

In a flash, the troll came back with the bull. The magnificent beast had drunk a river and was about to burst.

And burst it did!

Water poured all over the fire and soon the fire was out.

Frida was nearly home when she heard angry voices again. She turned and saw the trolls behind her on the path.

She cried, 'Oh, Bukolla, what can we do?'

For a third time, Bukolla said,

> Pluck a hair from my tail, dear girl, and lay it on the ground.

Frida plucked a long brown hair and laid it on the grass.

The magic cow said to the hair,

Hair, turn into a mountain so high That only a bird can pass you by.

At that instant, a mighty mountain blocked the path between Frida and the trolls.

The smaller troll howled with rage when she saw the mountain.

But her big sister said, 'I have an idea. Run to our cave as fast as you can and bring back hammers and picks.'

The tiny troll did as she was told. In the blink of an eye, she came back. She was carrying the hammers and picks.

Then the sisters began to tunnel through the rock. Their tunnel got deeper and deeper, and narrower and narrower …

... until the walls were so tight that the trolls got stuck! They could not move forwards. They could not move back. They shouted and cried but it made no difference. And that is where they stay to this very day.

So Frida and Bukolla arrived home safely. Frida's parents greeted them warmly. They were delighted to see their cow.

They were quite pleased to see Frida, too.